I0121932

Gratitude to the Natural World

*Greetings, Commentaries, Reflections, and Activities
for Children, Families, and Classrooms*

by

Dr. Maria Delia Crosby, DNP

LOVINGKINDNESS PUBLICATIONS LLC
BRONX, NY, USA

Copyright © 2025 Lovingkindness Publications LLC
Text and original commentary © Dr. Maria Delia Crosby
Illustrations © Maria Delia Crosby

All rights reserved.
No part of this publication may be reproduced in any form without written permission from the publisher, except for brief quotations in reviews or scholarly works.

This book is inspired by the Thanksgiving Address: *Greetings to the Natural World*, a traditional Haudenosaunee (Six Nations) teaching. (General & Sara, n.d.) As we offer thanks, we remember the wisdom of the Haudenosaunee: "When we put our minds together as one family, we find peace in all our hearts." We share this teaching with deep appreciation and respect.

All activities and commentary are provided for educational purposes only.

For information, permissions, or inquiries, contact:
Lovingkindness Publications LLC
randolin1@gmail.com

First Edition

ISBN: 979-8-9938814-0-9

Library of Congress Control Number: 2025923754

Free Companion Guide for Teachers and Parents , download it here:
https://drive.google.com/file/d/1uWihrIxEmZ0pCSjs2AvWpwKfdUcpuokv/view?usp=sharing

For

Patricia Ann Smith,

a beloved mother-in-law, writer, poet, musician, and teacher.

She devoted her life to helping children grow, dream, and shine.

With gratitude for her steady guidance and joyful spirit.

— ❋ —

Table of Contents

Introduction

*E*very morning, the world wakes with us. The sun rises, birds sing, water flows, and trees breathe. Take a deep breath and picture the sun on your skin, the breeze on your face, and the ground beneath you. The Haudenosaunee people begin each day with thanks, reminding us we live among nature's treasures (Haudenosaunee Guide for Educators, n.d.; Words Spoken Before All Others, 2018).

In this book, we follow their way of greeting the world with grateful hearts. We will thank people, the Earth, the waters, and every being that helps life go on.

Read this book slowly, out loud, and together. After each greeting, pause to reflect or share your gratitude. Express thanks through a short song, a gentle movement, or a drawing. Use the commentaries and activities to notice your connections to each other, the Earth, and all living things.

Use this book in the classroom, at bedtime, or during morning circles. May it bring peace to your heart and harmony to your day.

Together, may we give thanks for the natural world and for our place in it.

Our minds are one

The People

Greetings

We gather as one family to celebrate life and the bonds that connect us. Each new day is a chance to show kindness to our families, friends, and even people we haven't met. Kindness helps make the world happier for everyone. With thankful hearts, we send warm greetings to everyone around us.

Commentary

We are all connected. Family, friends, teachers, and neighbors support our growth. The Thanksgiving Address starts with the human family, reminding us that respect and peace bring unity. Kindness creates belonging and daily peace. We share a duty to uplift each other by giving back through our time, talents, and care.

Reflection

Let kindness guide your thoughts, words, and actions today. Decide on one specific thing you will do to help someone feel included, happy, or cared for (for example, inviting someone to play or giving a compliment). Do this action today. Afterwards, reflect on how it made you and the other person feel by writing, drawing, or talking about what you learned.

Mother Earth

Greetings

We thank Mother Earth for food, water, and a loving home. She cares for us as we play and grow. Her gifts, flowers, trees, animals, and beautiful places, fill our lives. With love, we thank Mother Earth.

Commentary

Mother Earth is our living home and a wise teacher, nurturing all (Haudenosaunee Thanksgiving Address, n.d.). Her soil, water, trees, and animals provide what we need (Haudenosaunee Thanksgiving Address, n.d.). By caring for soil, plants, and water, we sustain life. She gives countless gifts, asking only kindness and respect in return. To turn gratitude into action, families can adopt daily habits, such as composting or reducing plastic use, to help protect Earth's resources.

Reflection

Choose one action today to help Mother Earth (pick up litter, plant a seed, or save water). Complete your action, then think about how it helped the Earth and how you feel. Write, draw, or talk about your experience.

The Waters

Greetings

We thank all waters, including rain, rivers, lakes, puddles, and oceans, for sparkling and flowing. Water quenches thirst, grows gardens, and lets us play and explore. Water moves through clouds, soil, roots, and life, bringing energy everywhere. We are part of water's endless journey, like drops in the sea. With thankful hearts, we thank water for its many gifts.

Commentary

Water fills our glasses, our food, and the puddles we splash in. It forms rain, snow, rivers, and us. When we protect water, we protect all life. Water unites us, and small actions matter.

Reflection

Pick a way to use water in a fun or helpful way (water a plant, play with water, or take a short shower). Afterward, think about how you used water and what you can do to keep it clean. Write, draw, or share your ideas.

The Fish

Greetings

We thank all fish and water-dwelling creatures, such as minnows, turtles, and frogs. They help keep water clean and healthy for all. They swim and wiggle, bringing balance and life to their home. For their gifts, we thank fish and water friends.

Commentary

Fish and water creatures keep our waters vibrant with life (Haudenosaunee Thanksgiving Address, n.d.). Observing them teaches us patience, teamwork, and appreciation for each individual. Caring for fish and their habitats supports a healthy planet. Let's focus on local fish; can you name any? By protecting them, we strengthen our connection to nature and honor our ecosystems.

Reflection

Choose one action to help fish and water creatures have a clean home (don't litter near water, talk about the importance of clean rivers, or be gentle with aquatic animals). Do this action today and notice what happens. Reflect on how your choice helps water animals. Write, draw, or talk about what you did.

The Plants

Greetings

We turn our thoughts to all the plants that grow upon the Earth. Every leaf, flower, and blade of grass works quietly to fill the world with beauty and life. The plants feed and shelter many beings, sharing their gifts with all. With thankful hearts, we give our greetings to the plants and hope their green life continues for generations to come.

Commentary

Plants turn sunlight into life, sharing their energy with all who depend on them. The Haudenosaunee tell of the Three Sisters who support one another; corn stands tall, beans climb, and squash covers the ground. Together, they remind us that cooperation helps all life to flourish. The plants also teach us quiet generosity. They give without judgment or asking in return, offering food, shade, medicine, and beauty to every living being. Each seed they send into the soil is a promise of life continuing. When we care for the plants and grow them with respect, we join their circle of giving and help the Earth stay green and alive.

Reflection

Imagine you are a plant. What gifts would you give to people, animals, or the Earth; food, shade, shelter, or beauty? Draw or write your answer and share it.

The Food Plants

Greetings

With thanks, we honor food plants such as corn, beans, squash, potatoes, and berries that help us grow strong. Grains and vegetables give us energy to learn and grow. Food plants feed people, animals, insects, and birds. We thank food plants for helping life continue and providing delicious food.

Commentary

Food plants show care and generosity. Each seed needs sunshine, rain, and support. Their grains, beans, berries, and roots nourish all. Harvesting and sharing food with thanks honors these gifts and supports health. To connect with these gifts, families can prepare a meal together. Choose a recipe with seasonal ingredients, gather, cook, and express thanks while eating. This ritual deepens bonds and roots gratitude in shared experience.

Reflection

Choose a food plant you'd like to grow for your family or community. Who would you share it with, and why? Draw or write your answer, then share and discuss.

The Medicine Herbs

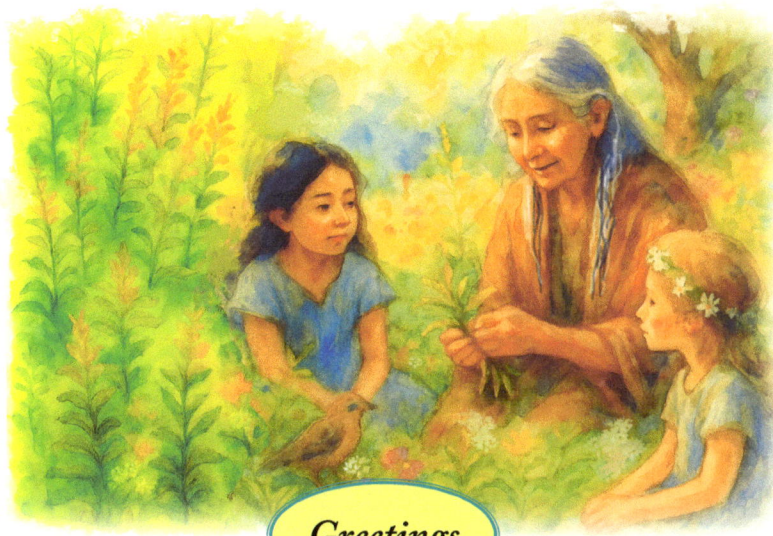

Greetings

We thank all healing plants such as herbs, leaves, roots, and flowers that help us feel better. These plants comfort and heal us. They grow quietly, offering gentle care to those in need. We are thankful for the wisdom shared about healing plants. We are thankful for healing plants and those who know their gifts.

Commentary

Healing plants show us that nature cares for everyone. Their leaves, roots, and flowers can make teas, medicines, or soothing balms. People who learn about these plants are careful and patient, listening to nature. We acknowledge and give thanks to the local healers and elders who hold and share this wisdom with respect and care. These knowledge keepers remind us that understanding and wisdom are treasures to be cherished and shared. By honoring them, children learn that knowledge has both caretakers and sources. When we care for healing plants, they can continue to share their gifts with the world.

Reflection

Think of something or someone that helps you feel better when you're hurt or not feeling well. How could you use those ideas or actions to help someone else feel cared for? Plan your idea and share it with a friend or family member.

The Animals

Greetings

Let's thank all animals, big and small, wild and tame. Animals live everywhere, each with unique gifts such as the fox's cleverness, the rabbit's speed, or the owl's eyes. Animals share the Earth with us and teach harmony. Every animal, no matter how small, matters. We are grateful for all the amazing animals, and we hope they will always have safe places to live and plenty of room to roam.

Commentary

Animals remind us that we are all part of one big Earth family. Each animal has something special to share, like the deer is gentle, the bear is brave, and the turtle is patient. The Haudenosaunee worldview regards animals as relatives, reflecting a profound connection and respect for them as part of the human family (Haudenosaunee Thanksgiving Address, n.d.). When we watch animals and treat them kindly, we can learn about courage, patience, and how to care for others. When we respect animals, we help create a world where everyone, people and animals, can live together happily.

Reflection

What is something you have learned from watching an animal? How can you treat animals with kindness every day?

The Trees

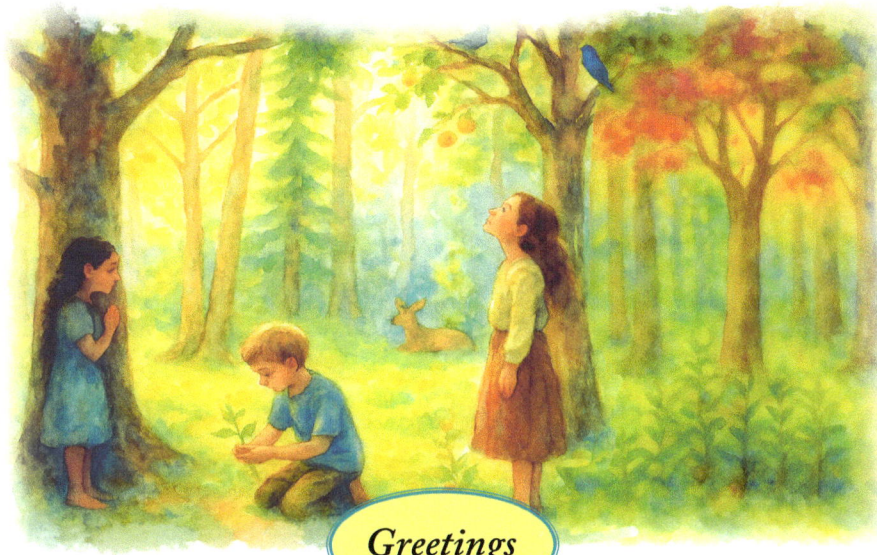

Greetings

Let's turn our minds and hearts to the trees, the giant family standing tall all over the Earth. Every kind of tree has its own special gifts. Some give us apples or oranges to eat, others give us cool shade, branches to climb, or homes for birds and squirrels. Tree roots hold the dirt steady so it doesn't wash away, and their branches reach high into the sky, reminding us to stand tall and be strong. With thankful hearts, we send our warmest greetings and biggest thanks to all the trees everywhere.

Commentary

Trees teach us to be patient and generous as they grow through every season, sharing their shade, fruit, and branches with everyone. Their roots keep the ground steady, and their branches reach up for the light. To learn more from trees, choose one to observe over time. Keep a simple journal to record your observations or create a time-lapse photo collection to capture changes. These activities will help you improve your observation skills and notice how the tree responds to the world around it. By following a tree's growth, you can form a lasting relationship with nature.

Reflection

What is one way you can share your talents or kindness with others, just like trees share their gifts with everyone?

The Birds

Greetings

Let's bring our minds and hearts together to thank all the birds, tiny and big, who fill the sky with life and beautiful songs. From the tiniest sparrow to the great eagle, every bird reminds us to start each morning with joy and hope. Their songs lift our hearts and remind us how wonderful it is to be alive. We send our warmest greetings and biggest thanks to all the birds of the world.

Commentary

Birds show us how to welcome each day with a happy heart. Their songs are gifts that fill the air with music and hope. Even before we wake up, birds are already singing to greet the sunrise and say thank you for a new day. From the eagle flying high above to the little birds close to home, each one has its own special song. When we listen carefully, the birds help us remember that every day is a gift, and being thankful is like singing a song in our hearts.

Reflection

If you could join the birds' morning song, what would your song of thanks be about? Try singing or saying your own words of gratitude out loud!

The Four Winds

Greetings

We give thanks to the Four Winds that move through the world, blowing gently or strongly from the east, south, west, and north. These winds come from all around us, carrying fresh air and bringing the changing seasons, such as spring, summer, fall, and winter. The winds sing and whistle in the air, cool us on hot days, and help move clouds across the sky so that changes can begin. With grateful hearts, we send our warmest thanks to the Four Winds for their gifts all year long.

Commentary

The winds show us that life is always moving and changing. We can't see the wind, but we can feel it on our faces or hear it in the trees. Winds bring rain to help plants grow and move clouds, so we get sunshine or shade. Each wind brings a new season—spring's warm breezes that signal planting time, summer's gentle air that encourages growth and play, autumn's cool gusts that remind us of harvest, and winter's chilly winds that invite rest and reflection. The winds personify the tasks and changes each season requires, anchoring them in our collective memory. They remind us that change can be good, and each new season has special gifts for everyone.

Reflection

What is your favorite season, and how does the wind help make it special? Can you think of a time when a change, such as the arrival of a new season, brought something good?

17

The Thunderers

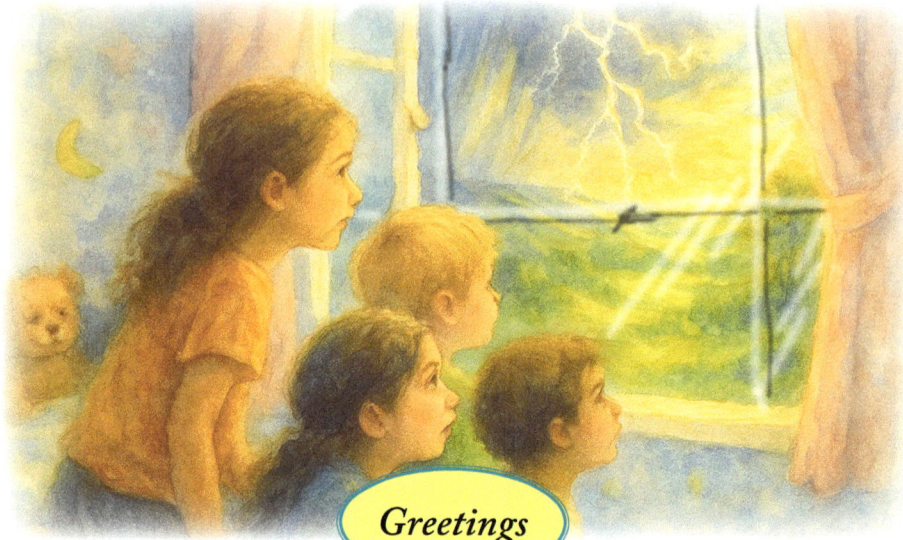

Greetings

Let's turn our thoughts to the Thunder Beings, our Grandfathers, who live in the west and fill the sky with their powerful voices. With their bright flashes of lightning and booming thunder, they bring the rain that helps everything grow fresh and new. Their power helps protect the world and keep everything in balance, making sure plants, animals, and people have what they need. With thankful hearts, we send our warmest greetings and biggest thanks to our Grandfathers, the Thunderers.

Commentary

The Thunderers show us that you can be strong and gentle at the same time. Their loud thunder brings the rain that helps plants grow, and their bright lightning wakes up seeds sleeping in the soil. While we admire their power, it's also important to seek shelter and stay safe when storms are approaching. Finding a safe place indoors during thunderstorms helps us respect the might of these natural forces while caring for our well-being. Even though their voices sound big and powerful, they use their strength to help and protect the Earth. The Thunderers teach us that real strength means taking care of others and helping the world stay safe and healthy.

Reflection

What is one way you can use your strength to help or care for someone, just like the Thunderers do for the Earth?

The Sun

Greetings

Let's give thanks to our Elder Brother, the Sun, who rises every morning to fill our world with bright, warm light. He travels from east to west across the sky, never missing a day, warming the Earth and waking up plants, animals, and people. His light reminds us to live with joy and to share our kindness and warmth with everyone we meet. With thankful hearts, we send our biggest thanks and warmest greetings to our Brother, the Sun.

Commentary

The Sun shows us what it means to give every day. He rises each morning and shares his warmth and light with the whole world, helping plants grow, animals play, and people feel happy. No matter where we live, the Sun's light reaches us all. He teaches us to be dependable and generous, encouraging us to share our kindness wherever we go so that everyone can grow and shine, too.

Reflection

What is one way you can bring kindness or cheer to someone's day, just like the Sun brings light and warmth to us all?

Grandmother Moon

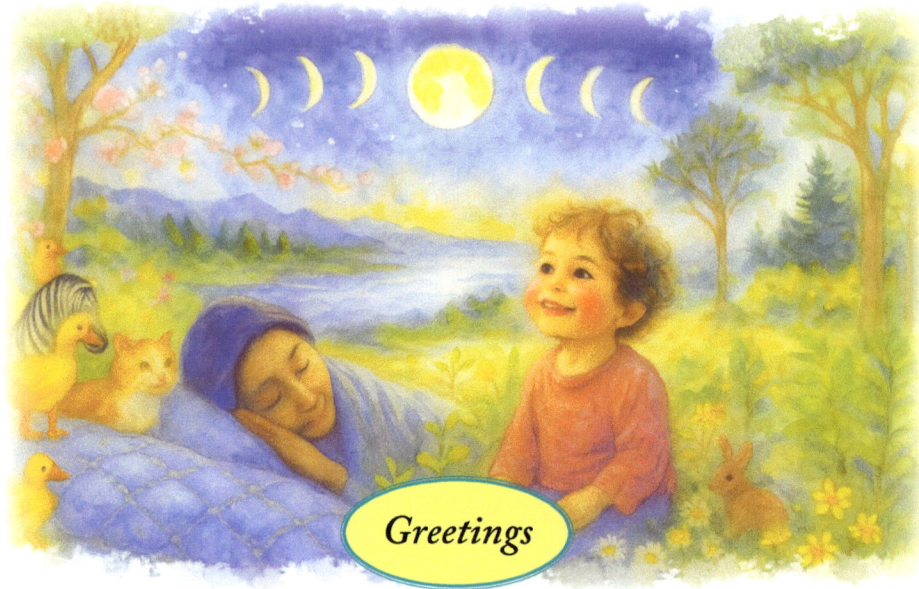

Greetings

Let's give thanks to our Grandmother the Moon, who lights up the night sky with her soft, gentle glow. She helps guide the rhythms of the oceans and lakes, and she is connected to the hearts of women everywhere. Her changing face helps us tell time and reminds us that everything in life has cycles—like being born, growing, resting, and starting again. She watches over new life as it begins, blessing the arrival of babies and new beginnings on Earth. With thankful hearts, we send our warmest thanks and greetings to our Grandmother, the Moon.

Commentary

Grandmother Moon teaches us to go with the flow and notice how life changes in cycles. Each night, her shape changes, from a tiny sliver to a full round moon and back again, showing us that every part of a cycle has its own beauty. She helps the oceans move with her pull and watches over us while we sleep, bringing peace and comfort. The Moon reminds us to be patient, to rest, and to find gentle strength inside ourselves.

Reflection

When you look at the changing Moon, how does it make you feel about changes or new beginnings in your own life?

The Stars

Greetings

Let's give thanks to the stars who twinkle high above us like tiny, sparkling jewels in the night sky. The stars keep Grandmother Moon company, helping to light up the dark and bringing a magical glow to the world below. Their sparkle reminds us to look up with wonder and hope, and that even small lights can help us find our way when things seem dark. With thankful hearts, we send our warmest greetings and biggest thanks to the stars above.

Commentary

The stars show us that even the tiniest lights can shine bright in the darkness. Each star is special, and together they make amazing patterns across the night sky. Their gentle glow comforts people who are traveling or dreaming, and helps everyone find their way home. The stars teach us to find beauty in quiet moments and to remember that our own special light, even if it feels small, can make a big difference for someone else.

Reflection

What is one way you can shine your light, such as by being kind, helpful, or a good friend, to make someone's day better?

The Enlightened Teachers

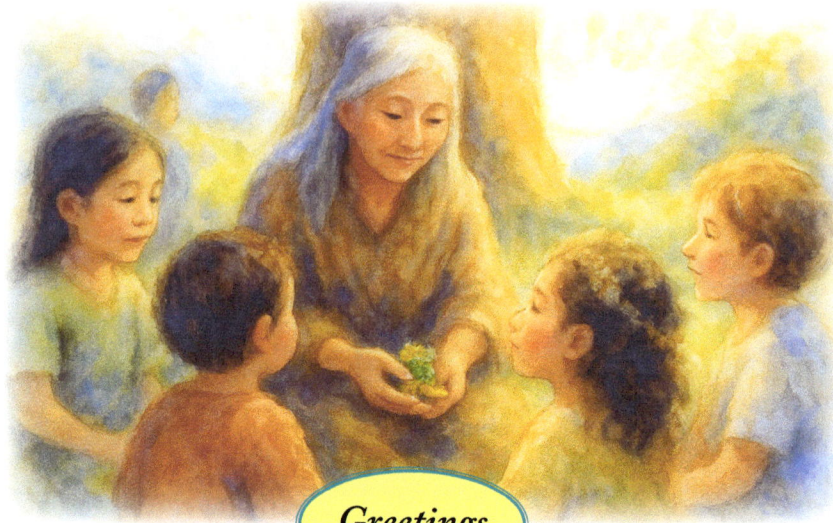

Greetings

Let's give thanks to all the Enlightened Teachers, wise people who help us learn, grow, and find our way. Whenever we forget how to be peaceful or kind, these teachers remind us to make good choices and care for others. Through their words, stories, and kindness, they help us remember that we are connected to everyone and everything around us. With thankful hearts, we send our biggest thanks and warm greetings to all the teachers who help us learn and grow every day.

Commentary

Enlightened teachers remind us that being wise means also being kind and caring. Their words are like gentle lights that help us find our way, especially when we feel lost or upset. They teach with patience, not by being the boss, but by showing us how to be our best selves. Teachers can be elders, healers, parents, or even friends who help us learn and grow. They show us that learning never ends and that sharing what we know with love can help everyone live in peace.

Reflection

Who is someone in your life who teaches you with kindness and care? What is something special you have learned from them?

The Creator

Greetings

Now let's turn our thoughts to the Creator, the Great Spirit who gives life and love to everything in the world. From this Earth we receive all that we need, including food, water, air, and love. Every gift of Creation reminds us that we are cared for every single day. With thankful hearts, we join our minds as one and send our biggest thanks to the Creator for all the wonderful gifts of life.

Commentary

The Creator helps us remember that we are cared for every moment. We are given everything we need, not just food, air, and water, but also the little miracles inside us. Our hearts beat, our lungs breathe, and our bodies grow, all without us even thinking about it. The same care that moves the rivers and the wind moves through us, connecting us to every part of the world. When we feel thankful, we remember that we are never alone because life itself is a special gift, given to us again and again.

Reflection

What are some things in your life that help you feel cared for or safe, even when you're not thinking about them? Who or what would you like to thank for these quiet gifts?

Closing Words

Greetings

Now we come to the end of our special words of thanks, but our gratitude can keep going every day. We have given thanks for the waters, the winds, the plants, the animals, and all our relatives in the circle of life. If there's anything we haven't remembered, you can add your own words of gratitude from your heart. Together, our minds and hearts are joined in thankfulness and peace.

Commentary

Gratitude never really ends. It grows every time we notice something good around us. These Thanksgiving Words remind us that everyone has their own special way to say thank you. Even if we haven't named every part of Creation, our hearts can hold them all. When we live with kindness and pay attention to the world, we help keep the circle of gratitude alive. Every thank-you, every caring action, helps make the world a more peaceful and loving place.

Reflection

What is something or someone you would like to give thanks for that we haven't mentioned yet? You can say your own words of thanks or draw a picture to share your gratitude.

Now our minds are one

After we finish giving thanks, let's take a quiet moment together. We can imagine all our thankful thoughts joining together, like little streams flowing into one big, peaceful river.

When we finish giving thanks, we take a moment of quiet. When many hearts are thankful at the same time, peace and happiness can grow and spread, just like water fills up a river. This is what people mean when they say, 'Now our minds are one.' It means we are connected by our gratitude and care for each other and the world. Take a moment to feel how good it is when everyone shares thankful thoughts together. That's the feeling of 'Now our minds are one.'

Commentary

You can close your eyes, sit quietly, and imagine your thank-you thoughts floating into the air, joining with the gratitude of people all around the world.

Reflection

How does it feel to know that lots of people are thankful at the same time as you? What changes inside you when you feel this big, peaceful togetherness?

Gratitude Journal

Keeping a gratitude journal can help you remember all the wonderful things in your life. You can use words or pictures to show what you're thankful for. There's no right or wrong way; just notice what makes your heart feel happy or grateful!

Use these pages to write, draw, or even doodle your own Thanksgiving Words. You can add to your journal any time you notice something special, big or small. You can answer with a sentence, a drawing, or both!

Today I'm thankful for _____
_____
_____
_____
_____.

Something in nature that makes me smile is_____
_____
_____
_____
_____.

Someone who helped me this week is _____
_____
_____
_____
_____.

One way I can care for the Earth is _____
_____
_____
_____
_____.

A sound that reminds me of happiness is _____
_____
_____
_____
_____.

If I could thank an animal or plant, I'd say _____
_____
_____
_____
_____.

The place where I feel most peaceful is_____
_____
_____
_____
_____.

A kind thing I did for someone was _____

_____

_____

_____

_____.

Something beautiful I saw outside was _____

_____

_____

_____

_____.

The weather today made me feel _____

_____

_____

_____

_____.

One thing I learned about nature is _____

_____

_____

_____

_____.

Create Your Own
Thanksgiving Words

**You can make your own Thanksgiving Words in any way you like!
Use your imagination and let your heart lead you.**

Try making your own song, poem, or story of thanks. You might want to start with: "I give thanks to…" and see what comes next. Think about what you are grateful for, maybe the sun for its warmth, a pet for their love, a tree for its shade, or your own hands for helping others. When you speak, write, or draw your thanks, you make the world's gratitude even bigger and brighter!

Activity Ideas:

1. Write a short poem, story, or letter of thanks to someone or something in nature.
2. Draw a picture showing all the things you are grateful for. There's no limit to what you can include!
3. Share your Thanksgiving Words by reading them out loud, acting them out, or showing your pictures to family, classmates, or friends.

Glossary & Learning Notes

Word	Meaning for Young Readers
Haudenosaunee	(pronounced: hoe-dee-no-SHOW-nee) – The name the people often called "Iroquois" use for themselves. It means "People of the Longhouse." The Haudenosaunee are a group of Native American nations in the northeastern part of North America, known for their wisdom, unity, and the Thanksgiving Address.
Thanksgiving Address	A special message or series of greetings from the Haudenosaunee people, spoken to give thanks for everything in the natural world. The Thanksgiving Address is often shared at the start and end of important gatherings. It helps everyone remember to be grateful for the earth, water, plants, animals, sun, moon, stars, and people.
Mother Earth	A way of talking about the planet we live on, as if the Earth is a caring mother who gives us everything we need: food, water, air, shelter, and beauty. Many Native peoples, including the Haudenosaunee, use the words "Mother Earth" to show respect and love for the land.
Harmony	When things work together peacefully. Example: Animals, plants, and people living together without fighting are in harmony.
Gratitude	The feeling of being thankful and showing it through words or actions.
Creator	The Great Spirit who made and connects all life.
Learning Notes	
Why Give Thanks?	Giving thanks helps us notice all the good things and people around us. It makes our hearts feel happier and helps us care for the world.
The Power of Words	Words can bring people together. When we share kind words or gratitude, we help everyone feel included and loved.
Nature as a Teacher	Plants, animals, the sun, the moon, and even the wind can teach us important lessons—like patience, sharing, and working together.
Sharing Gratitude	You can show gratitude in many ways: saying thank you, helping someone, drawing a picture, or just smiling at someone who needs it.
Everyone Can Join In	There's no right or wrong way to give thanks. You can do it quietly in your heart, with your family, or as a big group at school.

Author's Note and Acknowledgment

*T*his book is a new retelling inspired by the Thanksgiving Address: *Greetings to the Natural World*, shared by the Haudenosaunee (Six Nations) people and the Six Nations Indian Museum in Onchiota, New York.

I wrote these words with deep respect and gratitude for the Haudenosaunee, whose tradition of giving thanks reminds us all to live in balance with each other and with the Earth. My hope is that these pages will help children, families, teachers, and readers everywhere notice the many gifts around them and find their own ways to give thanks each day.

Thank you to the elders, teachers, and friends who have helped keep these traditions alive and who share their wisdom so generously. Special thanks to the families and children who bring gratitude into the world with their hearts and voices.

Nya:wen (thank you) to the Haudenosaunee for their inspiration, teachings, and guidance.

Maria Delia Crosby

❧

References

Alliance for a Viable Future. (2020). Cherish our precious earth by giving thanks. https://www.allianceforaviablefuture.org/blog/2020/9/30/cherish-our-precious-earth-by-giving-thanks

Dance for All People. (n.d.). Haudenosaunee Thanksgiving Address – 8. https://danceforallpeople.com/haudenosaunee-thanksgiving-address/haudenosaunee-thanksgiving-address-8/

General, S. (n.d.). We give our thanks. https://www.sarageneral.com/books/we-give-our-thanks-new-release

Mohawk Valley Museums. (n.d.). Haudenosaunee Thanksgiving Address. https://mohawkvalleymuseums.us/writing-series/haudenosaunee-thanksgiving-address/

National Museum of the American Indian. (n.d.). Haudenosaunee guide for educators. https://americanindian.si.edu/sites/1/files/pdf/education/haudenosauneeguide.pdf

Unitarian Universalist Fellowship of Falmouth. (n.d.). Haudenosaunee Thanksgiving Address: Greetings to the natural world. https://uuffm.org/wp-content/uploads/2023/10/Haudenosaunee-Thanksgiving-Address.pdf

U.S. Army War College. (n.d.). Haudenosaunee Thanksgiving Address. https://warroom.armywarcollege.edu/articles/thanksgiving-2023/

www.ingramcontent.com/pod-product-compliance
Lightning Source LLC
Chambersburg PA
CBHW060857270326
41934CB00003B/179